EMANATIONAL EXPRESSIONS

EMANATIONAL EXPRESSIONS

Poems From the Kabbalistic Tree of Life

ALEJANDRO PEREZ

O'LEARY
PUBLISHING
The Influencer's Press

BONITA SPRINGS, FL

This book belongs to

With love from

Published in the United States by
O'Leary Publishing
www.olearypublishing.com

The views, information, or opinions expressed in this book are solely
those of the authors involved and do not necessarily represent those
of O'Leary Publishing, LLC.

ISBN: 978-1-952491-11-5 (print)
ISBN: 978-1-952491-12-2 (ebook)
Cataloging-in-Publication Data is on file with the Library of Congress.

Editing by Heather Davis Desrocher
Proofreading by Boris Boland
Illustrations by Jonathan Rambinintsoa
Cover and interior design by Jessica Angerstein

Printed in the United States of America

To all Kabbalists past, present, and future

TABLE OF
CONTENTS

GIFTS FROM THE TREE OF LIFE
ASCENSIONAL INSIGHTS

There are layers upon layers of meaning in Kabbalah, especially in its original language, Hebrew. The Zohar, the source of Kabbalah, was written in Aramaic, even though its knowledge and wisdom stems from ancient Hebrew. Kabbalah is a never-ending journey of transformation and expansion.

I could tell you many stories of how Universal Kabbalah has transformed my life, but you would probably not believe me. I could tell you how during my ascension a very kind soul gave me 22 of the 23 volumes of the Zohar, which could easily take a lifetime to read and comprehend. I could tell you how my income doubled or even tripled. I could tell you how magical my family life has been. Most amazing of all, I could tell you how this journey has brought me closer to God. How did I arrive here to have this amazing life? Here are the highlights of my journey and what led to the creation of this book.

Being born and raised in Cuba, I emigrated to the United States in 1995 when I was 12 years old. Leaving everything I knew to move to a new country and learn a new language was very challenging. However, I didn't have a choice. I had nowhere to go except forward. Eventually, English became second nature. I was able to read and write without first translating it in my head. Occasionally, I would write about love, hate, light, and darkness, as rhyming words popped into my head. Thus, the poet in me was born.

During my school years, I disliked reading and writing. I remember choosing the smallest book possible for the summer reading assignments. One of these books was about energy healing, and it opened the door to the world of the unseen; the world of energies, chakras, and beyond.

I've been learning, practicing, and experimenting with energy since my teenage years. I could feel it in my body, flowing, and heating up. I remember meditating in the living room once and driving my mom crazy, because the rest of the house was cool and the spot where I meditated was warmer. I remember her asking why it was so warm where I was sitting. I chuckled inside, but I was not sure she'd understand if I told her what I was doing.

It was soon after high school that I became serious about learning more about energy healing. I found a Reiki teacher near my home in Miami. She held classes about the 72 divine names of

God and other practices that fascinated me. Little did I know it was Kabbalah. The things she taught were so clear to me. They made total sense. It was as if I was remembering something I already knew, not like I was learning something new.

It wasn't until I became an initiate in the lineage of King Salomon through the Modern Mystery School, and took Universal Kabbalah in 2018, that I connected the dots. I realized the seeds that had been planted all those years before had grown into the roots of my experience now.

Ascending the Tree of Life in Universal Kabbalah for the first time was amazing, especially the bottom and middle sections of the tree. Around the sefirot of Hod and Netzach, words and sentences would form in my head as I learned about each sefira. These words became poems.

The top three sefirot were more challenging for me. The words were increasingly difficult to grasp in the higher part of the tree and I was unable to complete the poems. It wasn't until my wife ascended the tree her second time, and energetically dragged me with her, that the poems for the remaining three sefirot (Chokmah, Binah, and Kether) were completed.

I shared these poems with my Kabbalah group as they came to me, and I found that my fellow Kabbalists in training enjoyed reading them. I hadn't thought about putting the poems into book format at that time. It was more an expression of my inner journey and I was simply sharing with the group as they shared with me.

However, when I finished the remaining poems, the idea to create this book came to me – and I almost talked myself out of it. I have a bad habit of giving up before I even start, often coming up with perfectly good excuses to back out or not do something that pushes me out of my comfort zone. The fear of failure often overwhelms me and I become stuck. But thanks to God and Kabbalah helping me break through this fear, and to a fellow kabbalist who works in publishing, I chose to create this book. Not only will you find meaning within its words, but also within its images that have been custom-designed just for you. Enjoy!

LAMENT OF
MALKUTH

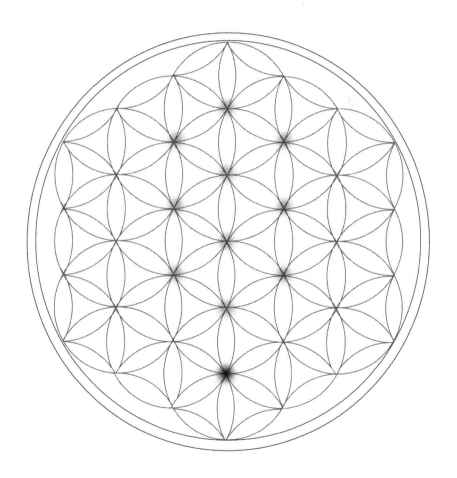

LAMENT OF
MALKUTH

I cry for my beloved

Our children have been cast

Outside of the kingdom

They fear they will not last

I shall be Adonai Ha-Aretz

In exile together with them

So they know they are not forgotten

Their love won't be in vain

For my husband loves me so

He yearns for my return

The gates he has opened

Lighting our way home

Much time has gone by

Many human years

Thy ascension as a race

Shall finally dry my tears

For then we shall return

To my beloved's embrace

When we finally ascend home

As a human race

REDEMPTION OF
YESOD

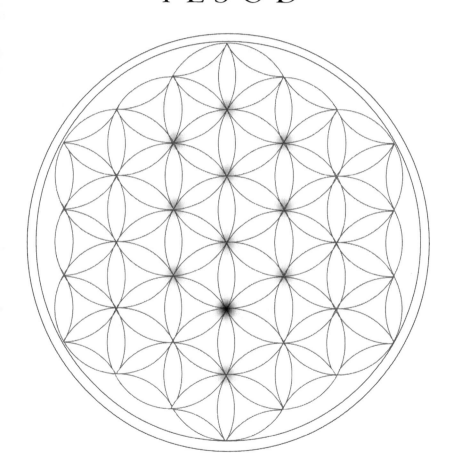

REDEMPTION OF
YESOD

Thou art forsaken it may seem

For through free will does thou devise

As a consequence of sin

Constructs of thy demise

But in me, Shaddai El Chai

In me thou shall confide

In the prism of my light

Thy true self thou cannot hide

Thou bare thy sin, thy past, thy all

And in repentance thou shall rise

Within my foundation from thy falls

Seeing through the falsehood of demise

Thou art eternal beings

And in eternity thou shall shine

Even when times are grim

Just remember thou art divine

ELATION OF
HOD

ELATION OF
HOD

Through the energy, the thoughts, the force

I now feel it to my core

Giving me some sort of form

Like a perfect storm

Through me, Elohim Tzabaoth

Akin to wearing a cloth

That which was the force of the storm

Begins to take on form

Let us prepare to manifest her desire

His thought born of fire

Fear not, my beautiful creations

Find the perfection within imperfections

For imperfection is but an illusion

An illusion of thy own creation

My creations are forever perfect

It is a matter of perception

Simply climb higher and higher

Along the path of liberation

Thou will find me in thee, and thee in me

Once thou reach thy destination

OSCILLATION OF
NETZACH

OSCILLATION OF
NETZACH

One language is universal

Among those who are conscious

Whether be conquered, or be its conqueror

The universal language is emotion

Come to me, Jehovah Tzabaoth

Do not live from whim to whim

Do not let that which is without

Control that which is within

Fear not the pendulum of polarity

At one side discontent, at the other delight

While others are thrust to and fro

Be the master of its flight

Become the master of within

Project thy glory to those without

Thy brothers and sisters live in pain

Worrying and believing I'm not about

Lift a rock, turn a leaf

Never think I'm not around

Feel my presence and my being

Both within and without

AGAPE OF
TIPHARETH

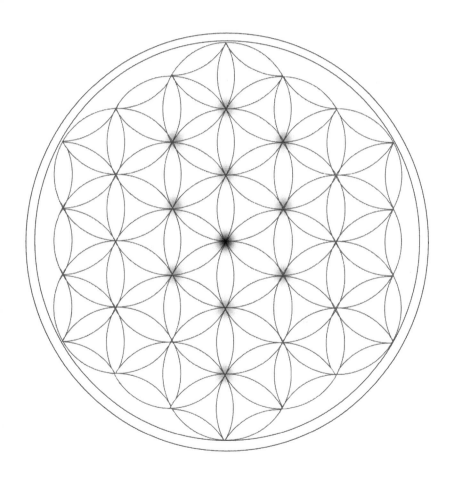

AGAPE OF
TIPHARETH

My net is cast far and wide

From the earth beyond the sky

See my beauty here and there

From our essence thou can't hide

In my presence, Jehovah Eloah Va-Daath

Like a child all the same

Whether mercy or judgment attained

Depends if by choice or circumstance thou came

I understand thy love

Although thou not mine

I love thine essence and thy being

Thy forms are all divine

I cradle thou, and cradle me

If our hearts of sun sublime

We unite within the light

Oh beautiful child of mine

Come in please, the door is open

See the beauty that I see

See the beauty that's in you

The same beauty that's in me

SHADOW OF
GEBURAH

SHADOW OF
GEBURAH

It is here that shadows cast

From the infinitely abundant light

The very first trace of form

Through severity thou shall find

It is in me, Elohim Gibor

Where light casts a shadowed form

I can see what serves and naught

What deforms and what adorns

Come up to me beautifully divine

Let me see thy true image

For in me thou shall confide

The true nature of thy visage

Cut away what no longer serves

Given what thou in truth desire

Up the tree thou may proceed

With a swing from the sword of fire

LIGHT OF
CHESED

LIGHT OF
CHESED

Limitless is my light

More permeating than the sun

Limitless I shine

Without a shadowed form

In me, El, thou shall find

Limitless mercy, love, and light

Do not fear the power of my shadowless form

Delight in the mercy my power provides

Oh limitless love for the sake of love

Oh limitless light for the sake of light

The bliss of endless giving

The abundance that I shine

Lift thy consciousness up the tree

Bathe in me, oh child of mine

Fill thy cup, thy vessel, thy being

With the shadowless, formless light

WHISPERS BENEATH
DAATH

WHISPERS BENEATH
DAATH

Hear the whispering thoughts

Coming from beneath Daath

They say it's not fair, they say react

They say do this, they say do that

Those unrelenting thoughts

That bring thou to thy knees

It's that penetrating voice

Pouring forth from the abyss

Its whispers familiar

With anxiety and fear

As they echo in thy head

It's thine own voice that thou hear

These fill thy hearts with false ideas

Thou call this free will

Programmed reactions of the mind

To steal, lie, profane, and kill

Realize the source of thy thoughts

Will thou choose the beast or the divine

Rise above the abyss beneath Daath

Cards on the table, we are out of time

GARMENT OF
BINAH

GARMENT OF
BINAH

In silent stillness I discern

Observe child, watch and learn

It is no easy task

Pierce the veil, remove thy mask

Things appear as this and that

That which matter, matter not

How can thou muster to understand

Holding out thy cupped hand

What thou see, and what thou hear

Isn't really what appears

The world of thought sure seems surreal

The mystery through which Jehovah Elohim reveals

Understand this, understand that

The mind is not where you think it's at

For true understanding comes from love

The boundless love from up above

BLESSING OF
CHOKMAH

BLESSING OF
CHOKMAH

Oh these beautiful stars I see

There in his blessing, Jah Jehovah I become

The Lord's mercy shines on me

To fill my bride with the blessing that I am

I am but a reflection

A glimmer of light from above

A glimmer of perfection

A glimmer of love

Love that dwells here

Forgiveness that vanquishes fear

Hear all who can hear

Forgiveness is what draws me near

KETHER

KETHER

בראשית

REFLECTIONS ON
KABBALAH

As I said at the beginning, there are layers upon layers of meaning in Kabbalah. And as you might find, there are layers of meaning in the words and images of this inspired book as well. My journey through the Tree of Life and Kabbalah has brought me closer to God than ever before. I hope that this book has enriched, and will continue to enrich, your journey as a Kabbalist.

In closing, I leave you with this. There was another tree in the garden of Eden. It was the Tree of Knowledge of Good and Evil. Why was it called this? Why wasn't it "the Tree of Knowledge" or "the Tree of Wisdom?" Why was it called the Tree of Knowledge of Good and Evil? Was the tree itself the vehicle through which we would experience the contrast between good and evil, obedience and disobedience?

In disobedience we would find death, but such is the cost of free will. To extinguish evil from the world is to extinguish free will. One must exist so the other can also. The universe is a place of polarity and balance, however, we can choose which direction to take, what to embody, in every moment. Shall we embody the attributes of the creator, as Adam did when he chose death so as not to abandon his beloved bride in her demise?

ACKNOWLEDGMENTS

I would like to thank my instructor, Eric Thompson, for bringing Universal Kabbalah to us in Naples, Florida. To my Guide, Barbara Segura, thank you for being there every step of the way through our ascension, and for guiding us to further understanding.

I am grateful to my fellow Kabbalists for their love and support, and to everyone at the Modern Mystery School, for everything they do.

Many thanks to my dear friend, fellow Kabbalist, and editor, Heather Davis Desrocher; and to my publisher, April O'Leary at O'Leary Publishing, for making this book possible. I'd also like to thank my mom for supporting my spiritual endeavors in my younger years.

And to my loving wife, Olayne Perez, thank you for being my companion and for helping bring to light parts of me that needed to heal and grow. Thank you for being my soulmate. And finally, I would like to thank the most high God without whom there would be nothing but an ocean of impossibility.

ABOUT THE
AUTHOR

Alejandro Perez, APRN, has been a nurse for many years, caring for people during the toughest times of their lives. While he understands the importance of physical health, he that knows spiritual health is equally important.

Alejandro is a Kabbalist, Life Activation Practitioner and an initiate in the Lineage of King Salomon. He is a bit of a workaholic, but when he's not working he spends time with his family, meditates, and reads or listens to audiobooks about God, energy, old world religions, and the world of the unseen. On long drives to visit his patients, Alejandro receives major downloads of insight and information. He received many of the words in these poems during those drives and other meditative states of mind, and in his dreams. Alejandro lives in Miami with his beautiful wife and his angelic children.

REFLECTIONS

REFLECTIONS

REFLECTIONS